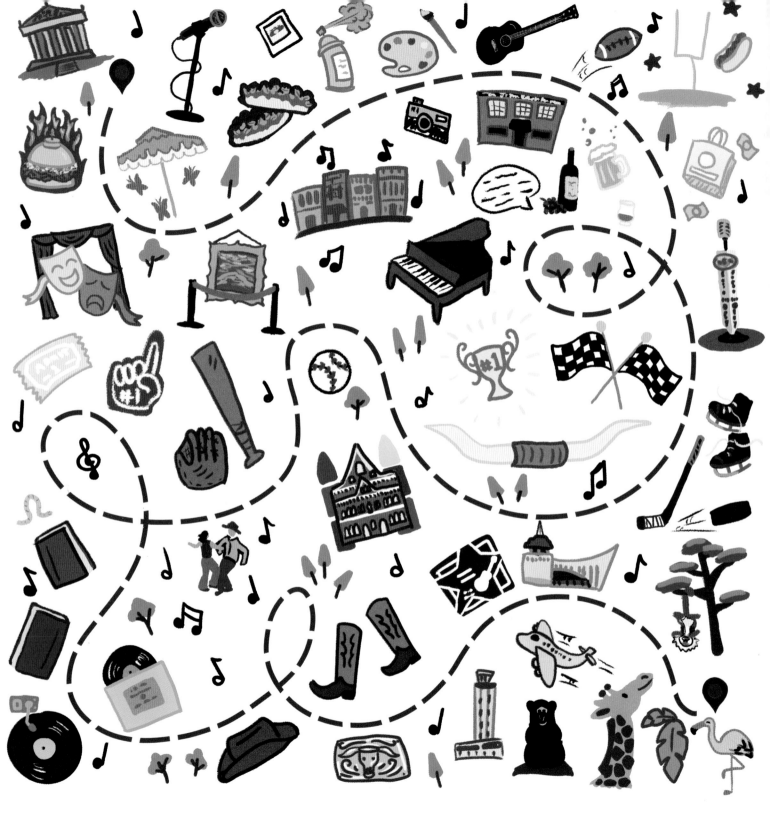

M is for Music City

The ABCs of Nashville

K.M. HIGGINBOTHAM
and ASHLYN E. INMAN
with NOAH PELTY

Illustrated by
BRIANNA YOUNGMAN

A PERMUTED PRESS BOOK
ISBN: 979-8-88845-150-2

M is for Music City:
The ABCs of Nashville
© 2023 by K. M. Higginbotham and Ashlyn E. Inman with Noah Pelty
Illustrated by Brianna Youngman
All Rights Reserved

Cover art by Brianna Youngman

Interior design by Kate Harris

Mural illustrations in this book have been recreated with the original artist's permission.

PERMUTED PRESS

Permuted Press, LLC
New York • Nashville
permutedpress.com

Published in the United States of America
1 2 3 4 5 6 7 8 9 10

To our Nashville

and its colorful, beautiful,

daring people.

You're one of a kind.

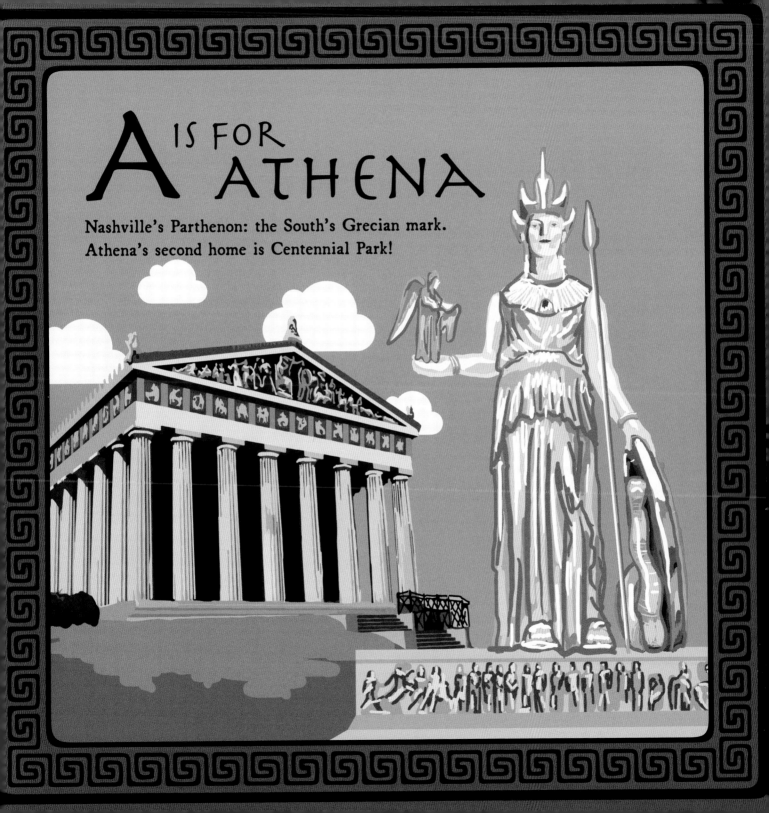

A IS FOR ATHENA

Nashville's Parthenon: the South's Grecian mark.
Athena's second home is Centennial Park!

B is for Bluebird

You know Taylor Swift?
She started out in this place!

Did you know? The idea of the "writers' round" was born at The Bluebird, but there are so many places around town where you can listen to music written by Nashville's up-and-coming songwriters!

So many great songs were born in this space.

C is for Chicken

"WOW!" YOU'LL CRY LOUDLY WHEN YOU TAKE YOUR FIRST BITE.

BUT NASHVILLE'S HOT CHICKEN IS A SOUTHERN DELIGHT!

Did you know that Prince's Hot Chicken recipe actually started off as a revenge plot? Thornton Prince was known for being a bit of a Casanova, and his slighted lover tried to get back at him by making his fried chicken extra spicy. Instead, she ignited an idea that would create Nashville's signature dish.

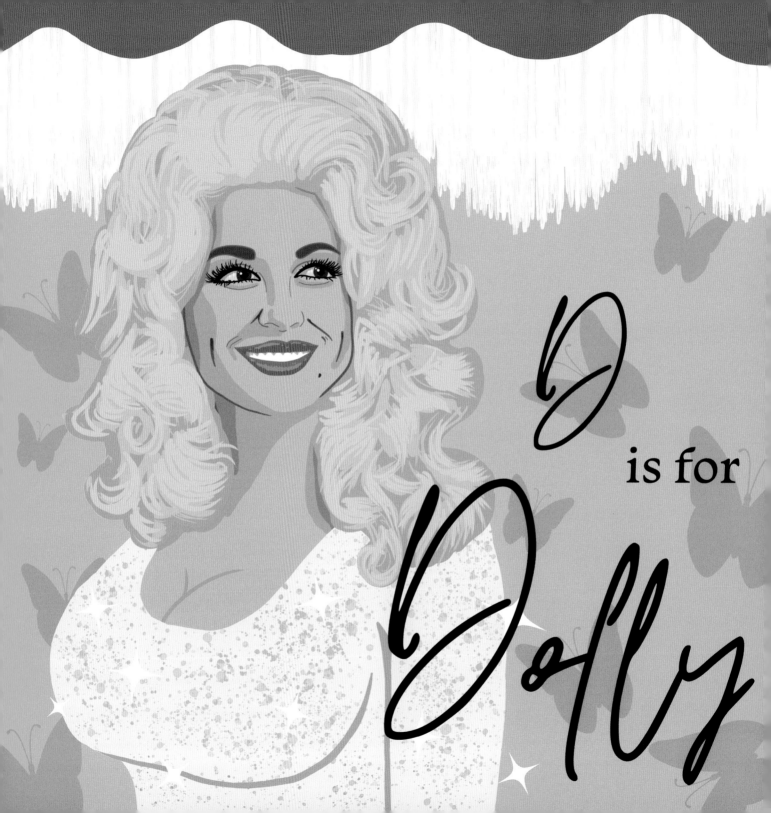

is for Dolly

Jolene went a'runnin
at a word from the Queen,
Nashville's chief songstress,
star of soundwaves and screen.

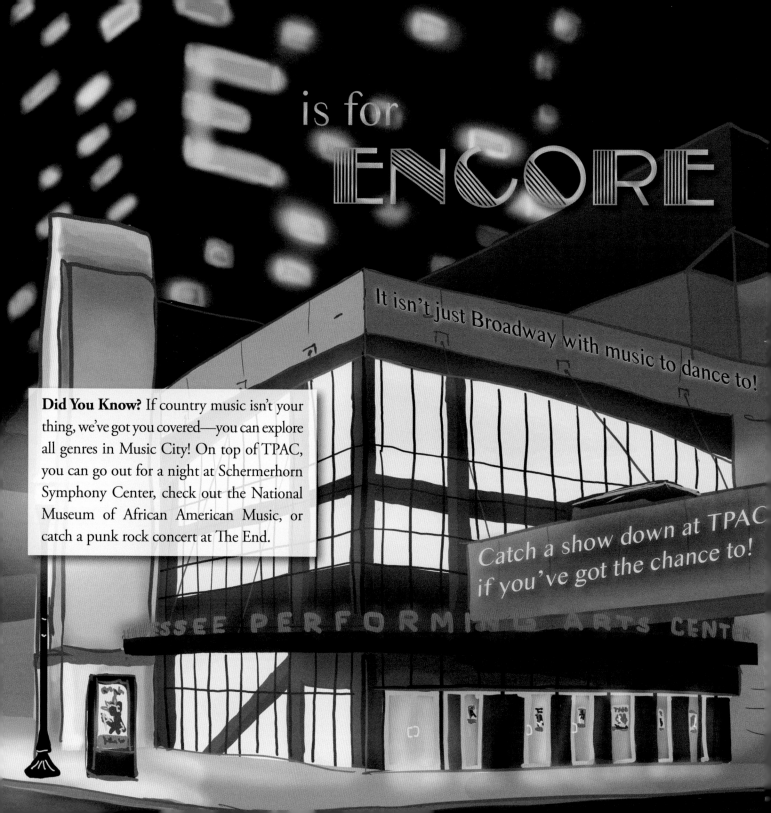

is for

ENCORE

It isn't just Broadway with music to dance to!

Did You Know? If country music isn't your thing, we've got you covered—you can explore all genres in Music City! On top of TPAC, you can go out for a night at Schermerhorn Symphony Center, check out the National Museum of African American Music, or catch a punk rock concert at The End.

Catch a show down at TPAC if you've got the chance to!

TENNESSEE PERFORMING ARTS CENTER

F is for

FRIST

If art museums are a must,
then we have just the thing.
The Frist hosts masters of all forms,
adorning every wing.

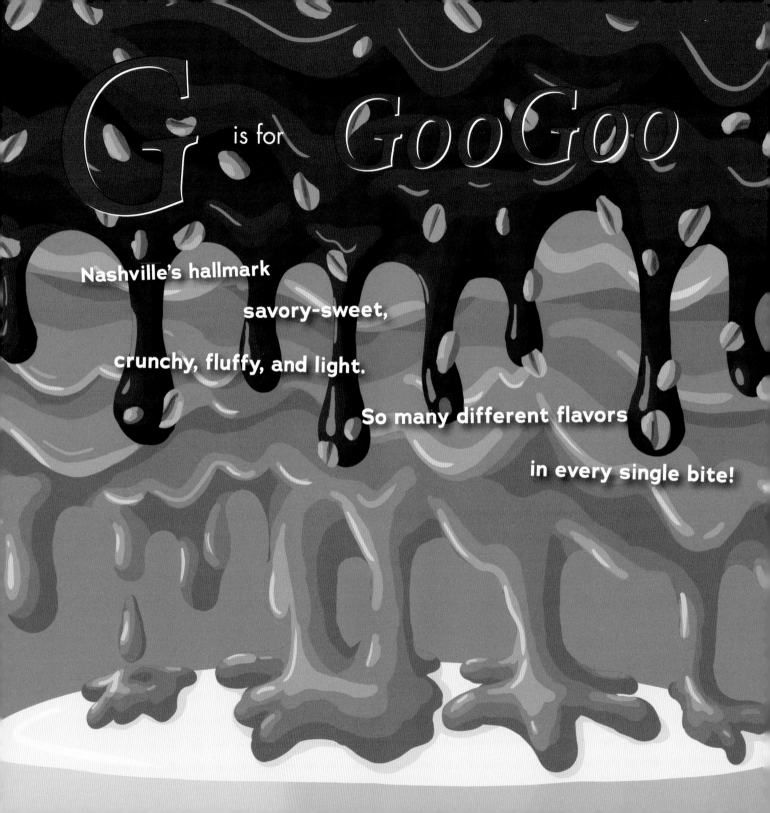

G is for GooGoo

Nashville's hallmark
savory-sweet,
crunchy, fluffy, and light.

So many different flavors
in every single bite!

 IS FOR

THE NEON LIGHTS
OF BROADWAY
ARE THE HEART
OF MUSIC CITY.

TO MISS
OUR FAMOUS
HONKY TONKS
WOULD SURE
BE A PITY.

ICONIC

KINDNESS IS

The Kind Way

HOME IS WHERE THE HEART IS

artist unkown

artist unkown

BORN IN TENNESSE

Eastside Murals

Eastside Murals

If you've looked us up on Instagram, you've seen our murals posted.

LOOKING PRETTY, MUSIC CITY

Emilly Eisenhart & Eastside Murals
Madewell

Donald "Drawbertson" Robertson

Kim Radford

Mark Palen

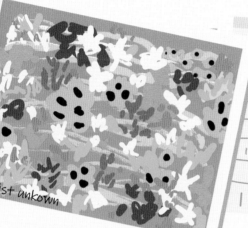

artist unkown

Joseph Ernst for
Paper & Pencil Co.

Andee Rudloff

IT'S gonna BE O.K.

Sarah Tate

Kelsey Montague

A perfect lasting
souvenir for all
the guests
we've hosted!

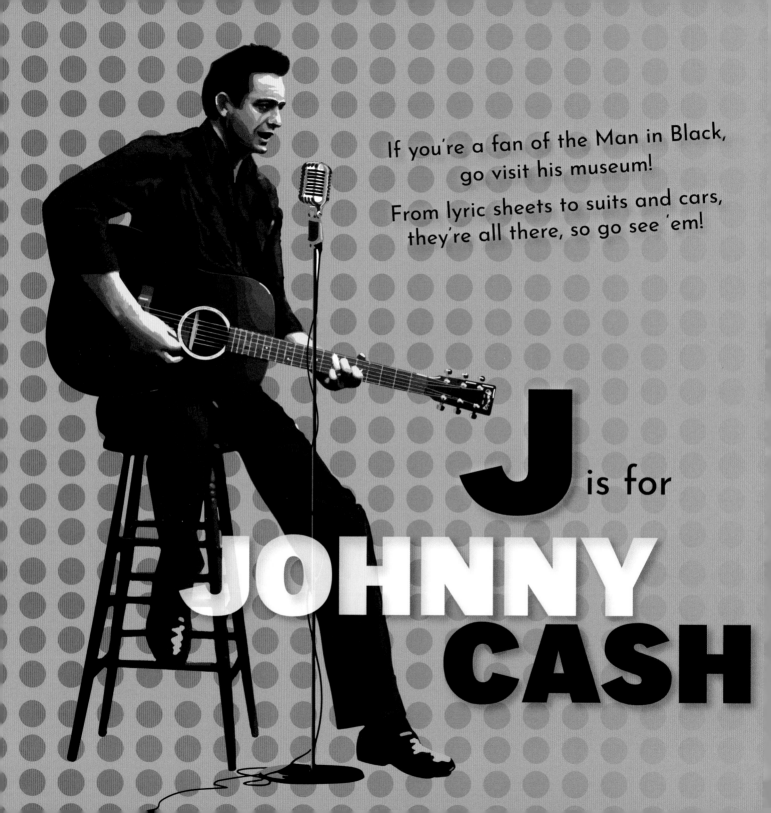

If you're a fan of the Man in Black,
go visit his museum!

From lyric sheets to suits and cars,
they're all there, so go see 'em!

J is for

JOHNNY
CASH

Titan up! Don gray and blue,
cheer on the Tri-Star team!

Our football fans are louder than most,
so be prepared to *scream!*

K is for KICK-OFF

If you're in doubt of where to go,
or what to see and do,

L is for

LOCAL

Ask a local!

We know all the sights,

both old and new!

Check out the back of the book for the best spots in Nashville!

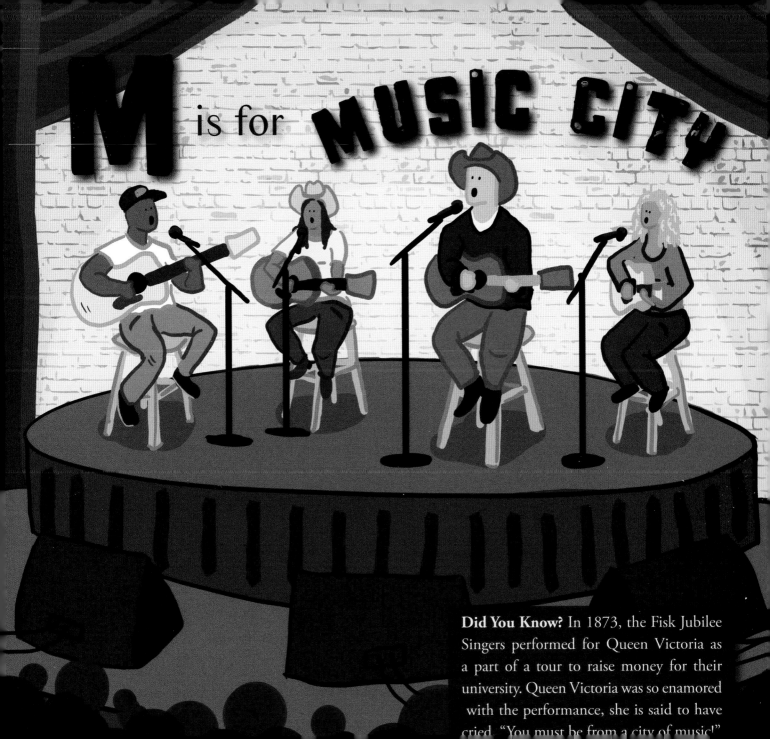

M is for MUSIC CITY

Did You Know? In 1873, the Fisk Jubilee Singers performed for Queen Victoria as a part of a tour to raise money for their university. Queen Victoria was so enamored with the performance, she is said to have cried, "You must be from a city of music!"

N is for **NASCAR**

Head to Nashville's Superspeedway

to watch the NASCAR Races!

If you like speed and a rowdy crowd,

this will cover all your bases!

O is for OPRY

"Hooooowdy!"

Minnie Pearl would cry at the top of every show.

And still today you'll see the ⬤ stars that everybody knows!

Did You Know that the iconic six-foot Circle on the Opry stage actually came from the Ryman? Before the Grand Ole Opry found its permanent home in 1974, their shows were held at the Ryman. The Circle honors the Opry's roots, and it is one of the highest honors in country music to be invited to join the Circle.

Grab a yellow jersey
and a hat to show your pride!
The Nashville Predators bring the heat,
though the cheering you'll provide

P is for PREDS

R is for RYMAN

The mother church of country music
has welcomed all the greats.

From R&B to rock and roll,

George Michael to George Strait!

Did You Know? The Ryman isn't called the "mother church" by chance—it was initially built as a church in 1892 and was converted into an auditorium in 1904.

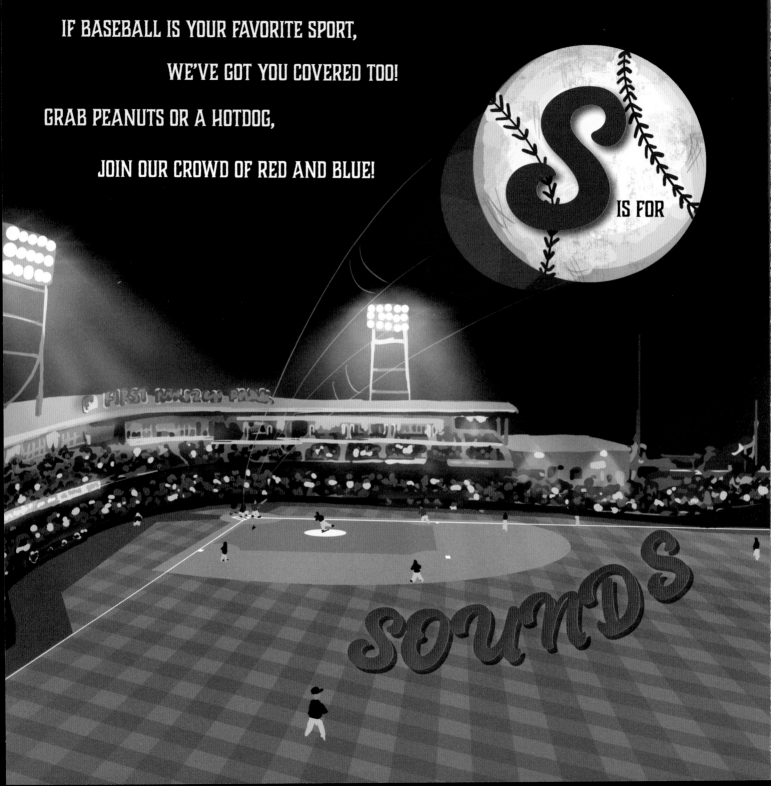

T is for TWO-STEP

It gets a little rowdy,

don't be scared to jump right in!

Just grab a partner,

say hello,

then you can start to spin.

U is for

University

Whether it's **BRUINS,**

COMMODORES,

BISONS,

or **TIGERS,**

Nashville's home to
lots of schools!
You'll find no
college finer.

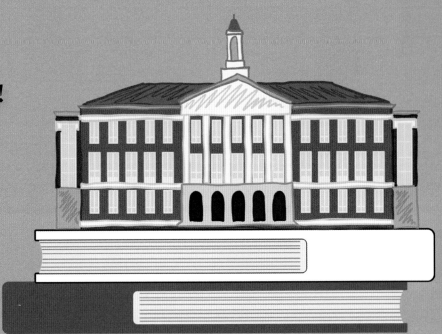

IF YOU PREFER TO JAM BY DROPPING NEEDLES ON A VINYL,

FROM THE GROOVE TO GRIMEY'S, WE'VE GOT ALL YOUR FAVORITE TITLES.

IS FOR V Vinyl

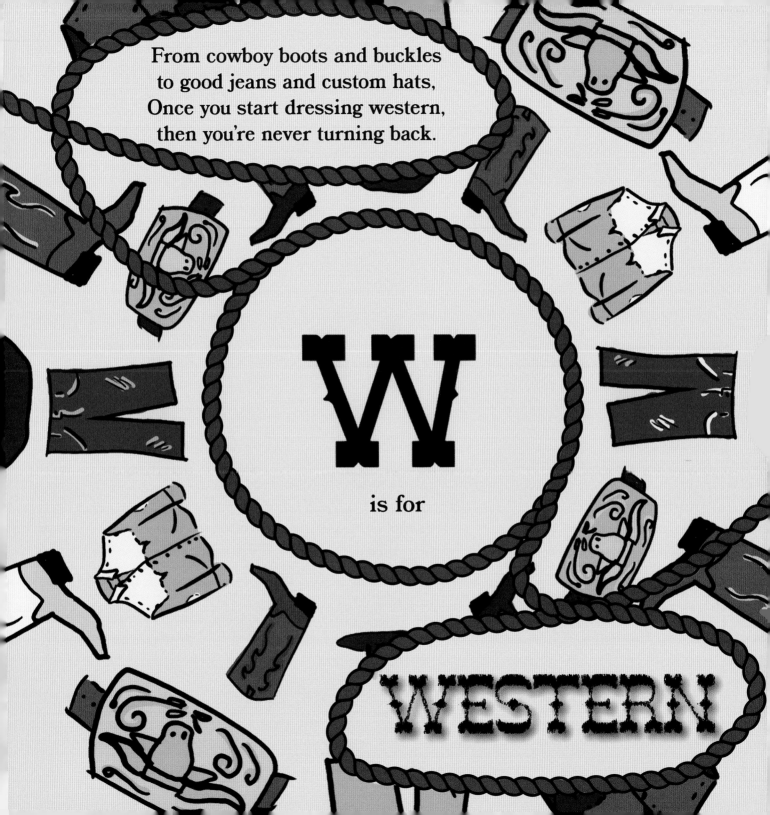

From cowboy boots and buckles
to good jeans and custom hats,
Once you start dressing western,
then you're never turning back.

W

is for

WESTERN

If you're about to come to town

to chase a neon dream,

do you have what it takes
to take on Nashville's music scene?

X is for

X-FACTOR

Y is for

You're Home

When you step off the plane
into the gates at BNA,
the famous carpet pattern's
the first sign you're home to stay.

It may be last, but it ain't least,
we've also got a zoo!
But did you know that here at ours
you can pet a kangaroo?

Our Favorite Spots in Nashville

This is in no way a complete list—it's difficult to only pick a few—
But this should give you a starting point when figuring out what to do.
Nashville is constantly growing, so there will always be new things to see.
Just be sure to check Google before beginning your journey.

Record Stores

Grimey's
1060 E Trinity Ln
Nashville, TN 37216
https://grimeys.com/

The Groove
1103 Calvin Ave
Nashville, TN 37206
https://thegroovenashville.com/

Luna Record Shop
230 Franklin Rd Ste 12D
Franklin, TN 37064
https://lunarecordshop.com/

Third Man Records
623 7th Ave S
Nashville, TN 37023
https://thirdmanrecords.com/

Vinyl Tap
2038 Greenwood Ave
Nashville, TN 37206
http://vinyltapnashville.com/

Bookstores

The Bookshop
1403 W Eastland Ave
Nashville, TN 37206
https://thebookshopnashville.com/

Bound Books
158 Front St Ste 106
Franklin, TN 37064
https://boundbookstn.com/

Elder's Bookstore
101 White Bridge Pk
Nashville, TN 37209
https://eldersbookstore.com/

Defunct Books
1108 Woodland St Unit A
Nashville, TN 37206
http://defunctbooks.com/

Fairytales Bookstore
1108 Woodland St Unit G
Nashville, TN 37206
https://fairytales
nashville.com/

McKay's Nashville
636 Old Hickory Blvd
Nashville, TN 37209
http://mckaybooks.com/

Parnassus Books
3900 Hillsboro Pk #14
Nashville, TN 37215
https://parnassusbooks.net/

Rhino Booksellers
4918 Charlotte Ave
Nashville, TN 37209
https://rhinobooksellers.com/

Specialty Retailers

Goo Goo Chocolate Co
116 3rd Ave S
Nashville, TN 37201
https://googoo.com/

Goodbuy Girls
1108 Woodland St Unit E
Nashville, TN 37206
https://goodbuygirls.com/

Hatch Show Print
224 Rep John Lewis Way S
Nashville, TN 37203
https://hatchshowprint.com/

Planet Cowboy
2905 12 Ave S
Nashville, TN 37204
https://planetcowboy.com/

Thunder Moon Collective
937 Woodland St
Nashville, TN 37206
https://thundermoon
collective.com/

White's Mercantile
2908 12th Ave S
Nashville, TN 37204
https://whitesmercantile.com/

Vintage & Antiques

Anaconda Vintage
1062 E Trinity Ln #101
Nashville, TN 37216
https://anacondavintage.com/

Backslide Vintage
4606 Gallatin Pk
Nashville, TN 37216
https://facebook.com/
backslidevintage/

Black Shag Vintage
1220 Gallatin Ave
Nashville, TN 37206
https://blackshagvintage.com/

East Nashville Antiques
3407 Gallatin Pk
Nashville, TN 37216
https://facebook.com/
eastnashvilleantiques

High Class Hillbilly
4604 Gallatin Pk
Nashville, TN 37216
https://highclasshillbilly.com/

The Hip Zipper Vintage
1008 Forrest Ave Ste A
Nashville, TN 37206
https://hipzipper.com/

Speakeasy Vintage
1102 Richmond Dr
Nashville, TN 37216
https://speakeasy
vintage.com/

Star Struck Vintage
604 Gallatin Ave #100
Nashville, TN 37206
https://starstruckvintage.com/

Music Stores

Carter Vintage Guitars
625 8th Ave S
Nashville, TN 37203
https://cartervintage.com/

Corner Music
3048 Dickerson Pk
Nashville, TN 37207
https://cornermusic.com/

Eastside Music Supply
2915 Gallatin Pk
Nashville, TN 37216
https://eastsidemusicsupply.com/

Fanny's House of Music
1101 Holly St
Nashville, TN 37206
https://fannyshouse
ofmusic.com/

The Gibson Garage
209 10th Ave S Ste 209
Nashville, TN 37203
https://gibson.com/
en-US/garage

Nashville Used & New Music
4876 Nolensville Pk
Nashville, TN 37211
https://nashvilleusedmusic.com/

Landmarks

Andrew Jackson's Hermitage
4580 Rachels Ln
Hermitage, TN 37076
https://thehermitage.com/

Bicentennial Capitol Mall State Park
600 James Robertson Pkwy
Nashville, TN 37243
https://tnstateparks.com/parks/
bicentennial-mall

Cheekwood Estate & Gardens
1200 Forrest Park Dr
Nashville, TN 37205
https://cheekwood.org/

Country Music Hall of Fame
222 Rep John Lewis Way S
Nashville, TN 37203
https://countrymusichallof
fame.org/

The Parthenon at Centennial Park
2500 West End Ave
Nashville, TN 37203
https://nashvilleparthenon.com/

Nashville Superspeedway
4847-F McCrary Rd
Lebanon, TN 37090
https://nashvillesuper
speedway.com/

Nashville Zoo at Grassmere
3777 Nolensville Pk
Nashville, TN 37211
https://nashvillezoo.org/

Tennessee State Capitol
600 Dr. MLK Jr Blvd
Nashville, TN 37243
https://tnmuseum.org/
state-capitol

Music Venues

The Basement East
917 Woodland St
Nashville, TN 37206
https://thebasementnashville.com/

The Bluebird Cafe
4104 Hillsboro Pk
Nashville, TN 37215
https://store.bluebirdcafe.com/

EXIT/IN
2208 Elliston Pl
Nashville, TN 37203
https://exitin.com/

Grand Ole Opry
2804 Opryland Dr
Nashville, TN 37214
https://opry.com/

Listening Room Cafe
618 4th Ave S
Nashville, TN 37210
https://listening
roomcafe.com/

Ryman Auditorium
116 5th Ave N
Nashville, TN 37219
https://ryman.com/

The End
2219 Elliston Pl
Nashville, TN 37203
https://endnashville.com/

Murals

"Flowers" by Unknown Artist
2900 12th Ave S
Nashville, TN 37204

"Arcade" by Eastside Murals
1721 21st Ave
Nashville, TN 37212
https://eastsidemuralco.com/

"Dragon" by Kim Radford
1224 Meridian St
Nashville, TN 37207
https://kimradfordart.com/

**"Drippy Lips" by Donald
"Drawbertson" Robertson**
1814 21st Avenue S
Nashville, TN 37212
https://donalddrawbertson.com/

**"Hillsboro Village"
by Andee Rudloff**
2013 Capers Ave
Nashville, TN 37212
https://chicnhair.com/

**"Home is Where the Heart Is"
by Unknown Artist**
1909 12th Ave S
Nashville, TN 37203
https://visitmusiccity.com/local-busi-
ness/home-where-heart-mural#

**"Hot Air Balloon"
by Kelsey Montague**
1034 West Eastland Ave
Nashville, TN 37206
https://kelseymontagueart.com/

"Import Flowers" by Mark Palen
3636 Murphy Rd
Nashville, TN 37209
https://palenart.com/

"It's Gonna Be OK" by Sarah Tate
3020 Charlotte Ave
Nashville, TN 37209
https://sarahtate.co/

**"Looking Pretty, Music City" by
Emily Eisenhart and
Eastside Murals**
2709 12th Ave S
Nashville, TN 37204
https://emilyeisenhart.com/
https://eastsidemuralco.com/

**"Love Y'all" by Joseph Ernst with
Pencil & Paper Co.**
2020 Lindell Ave
Nashville, TN 37203
https://joseph-ernst.com/
https://pencilandpaperco.com/

"The Tennessee Original"
by Eastside Murals
1000 Woodland St
Nashville, TN 37206
https://eastsidemuralco.com/

Sports Venues

Bridgestone Arena
501 Broadway
Nashville, TN 37203
https://bridgestonearena.com/

First Horizon Park
19 Jr Gilliam Way
Nashville, TN 37219
https://firsthorizonpark.com/

GEODIS Park
501 Benton Ave
Nashville, TN 37203
https://nashvillesc.com/
geodispark/

Nissan Stadium
1 Titans Way
Nashville, TN 37213
https://nissanstadium.com/

Art & Culture

Frist Art Museum
919 Broadway
Nashville, TN 37203
https://fristartmuseum.org/

Johnny Cash Museum
119 3rd Ave S
Nashville, TN 37201
https://johnnycash
museum.com/

National Museum of African
American Music
510 Broadway
Nashville, TN 37203
https://nmaam.org/

Schermerhorn Symphony Center
1 Symphony Pl
Nashville, TN 37201
https://nashville
symphony.org/

Tennessee Performing Arts
Center (TPAC)
505 Deadrick St
Nashville, TN 37243
https://tpac.org/

Colleges and Universities

American Baptist College
1800 Baptist World Center Dr
Nashville, TN 37207
https://abcnash.edu/

Belmont University
1900 Belmont Blvd
Nashville, TN 37212
https://belmont.edu/

Cumberland University
1 Cumberland Sq
Lebanon, TN 37087
https://cumberland.edu/

Fisk University
1000 17th Ave N
Nashville, TN 37208
https://fisk.edu/

Lipscomb University
1 University Park Dr
Nashville, TN 37204
https://lipscomb.edu/

Middle Tennessee State University
1301 E Main St
Murfreesboro, TN 37132
https://mtsu.edu/

Nashville State Community College
120 White Bridge Rd
Nashville, TN 37209
https://nscc.edu/

Nossi College of Art
590 Creative Way
Nashville, TN 37115
https://nossi.edu/

Tennessee State University
3500 John A Merritt Blvd
Nashville, TN 37209
https://tnstate.edu/

Trevecca Nazarene University
333 Murfreesboro Pk
Nashville, TN 37210
https://trevecca.edu/

Vanderbilt University
2201 West End Ave
Nashville, TN 37235
https://vanderbilt.edu/

Volunteer State Community
College
1480 Nashville Pk
Gallatin, TN 37066
https://volstate.edu/

Welch College
1045 Bison Trl
Gallatin, TN 37066
https://welch.edu/

Breweries, Distilleries, and Vineyards

Arrington Vineyards
6211 Patton Rd
Arrington, TN 37014
https://arringtonvineyards.com/

Bearded Iris Brewing
101 Van Buren St
Nashville, TN 37208
https://beardedirisbrewing.com/

Belle Meade Winery
5025 Harding Pk
Nashville, TN 37205
https://bellemeade
winery.com/

Big Machine Brewery & Distillery
122 3rd Ave S
Nashville, TN 37201
https://bigmachine
vodka.com/

Diskin Cider
1235 Martin St
Nashville, TN 37203
https://diskincider.com/

Jackalope Brewing Company
429B Houston St
Nashville, TN 37203
https://jackalopebrew.com/

Living Waters Brewing
1056 E Trinity Ln #101
Nashville, TN 37216
https://livingwaters
brewing.com/

New Heights Brewing
928 Rep John Lewis Way S
Nashville, TN 37203
https://newheights
brewing.com/

Ole Smoky & Yee-Haw Brewing
423 6th Ave S
Nashville, TN 37203
https://olesmoky.com/

Smith & Lentz Brewing and Pizza
903 Main St
Nashville, TN 37206
https://smithandlentz.com/

Southern Grist Brewing Company
754 Douglas Ave
Nashville, TN 37207
https://southerngrist
brewing.com/

Tennessee Brew Works
809 Ewing Ave
Nashville, TN 37203
https://tnbrew.com/

Nashville Hot Chicken

Bolton's Spicy Chicken and Fish
624 Main St
Nashville, TN 37206
https://boltonsspicy.com/

Hattie B's Hot Chicken
112 19th Ave S
Nashville, TN 37203
https://hattieb.com/

Prince's Hot Chicken
5814 Nolensville Pk
Nashville, TN 37211
https://princeshotchicken.com/

Red's 615 Kitchen
115 27th Ave N
Nashville, TN 37203
https://reds615kitchen.com/

About the Illustrator

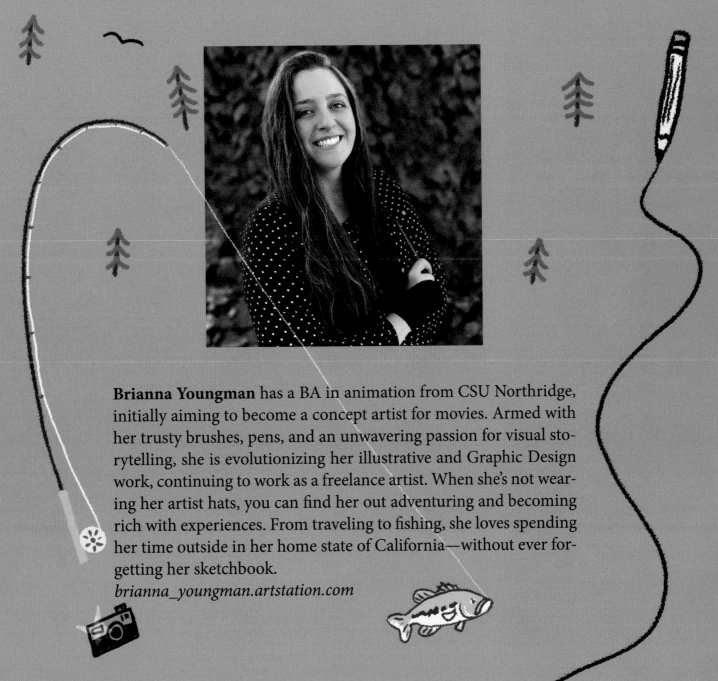

Brianna Youngman has a BA in animation from CSU Northridge, initially aiming to become a concept artist for movies. Armed with her trusty brushes, pens, and an unwavering passion for visual storytelling, she is evolutionizing her illustrative and Graphic Design work, continuing to work as a freelance artist. When she's not wearing her artist hats, you can find her out adventuring and becoming rich with experiences. From traveling to fishing, she loves spending her time outside in her home state of California—without ever forgetting her sketchbook.

brianna_youngman.artstation.com

About the Authors

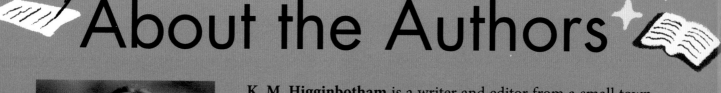

K. M. Higginbotham is a writer and editor from a small town in North Alabama. Her first novel debuted when she was sixteen years old. Since then, she has published two additional novels, started a freelance editing business, and chased a career in traditional publishing. She now resides in Nashville, where she spends most of her time working on creative ventures, reading too many books, and planning trips around the world with her husband.

kmhigginbotham.com

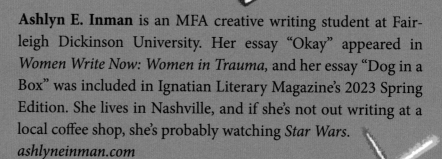

Ashlyn E. Inman is an MFA creative writing student at Fairleigh Dickinson University. Her essay "Okay" appeared in *Women Write Now: Women in Trauma,* and her essay "Dog in a Box" was included in Ignatian Literary Magazine's 2023 Spring Edition. She lives in Nashville, and if she's not out writing at a local coffee shop, she's probably watching *Star Wars.*

ashlyneinman.com

Noah Pelty is a songwriter living in Nashville, TN. His songs have been recorded by various artists across several genres. He spends his days writing new songs and performing with bands in Nashville and on the road.

@noahpelty